Predators

LEOPARD SEALS

BY MARISSA KIRKMAN

WWW.APEXEDITIONS.COM

Copyright © 2024 by Apex Editions, Mendota Heights, MN 55120. All rights reserved. No part of this book may be reproduced or utilized in any form or by any means without written permission from the publisher.

Apex is distributed by North Star Editions:
sales@northstareditions.com | 888-417-0195

Produced for Apex by Red Line Editorial.

Photographs ©: iStockphoto, cover, 8–9, 10–11, 16–17, 20, 26–27; Shutterstock Images, 1, 4–5, 6, 7, 12–13, 14–15, 19, 21, 22–23, 29; Michael Nolan/robertharding/Alamy, 24–25

Library of Congress Control Number: 2023910632

ISBN
978-1-63738-773-3 (hardcover)
978-1-63738-816-7 (paperback)
978-1-63738-897-6 (ebook pdf)
978-1-63738-859-4 (hosted ebook)

Printed in the United States of America
Mankato, MN
012024

NOTE TO PARENTS AND EDUCATORS

Apex books are designed to build literacy skills in striving readers. Exciting, high-interest content attracts and holds readers' attention. The text is carefully leveled to allow students to achieve success quickly. Additional features, such as bolded glossary words for difficult terms, help build comprehension.

CHAPTER 1
HUNTING IN THE COLD 4

CHAPTER 2
LEOPARD SEAL BODIES 10

CHAPTER 3
UNDERWATER HUNTERS 16

CHAPTER 4
LIFE OF A LEOPARD SEAL 22

COMPREHENSION QUESTIONS • 28
GLOSSARY • 30
TO LEARN MORE • 31
ABOUT THE AUTHOR • 31
INDEX • 32

CHAPTER 1

Hunting in the Cold

A group of penguins moves across the icy rocks. One penguin falls into the water. A hungry leopard seal is waiting nearby.

Leopard seals sometimes wait for penguins in shallow waters.

Leopard seals use their flippers to change directions while swimming.

The leopard seal rushes toward the penguin. Its **flippers** slice through the water.

DANGER UNDER THE ICE

Large ice sheets form above the sea in Antarctica. Leopard seals hunt near the edges. They chase penguins that come close. Sometimes they break through the ice and grab chicks.

Leopard seals are one of the only kinds of seal that hunt penguins.

The seal bites the penguin with its strong jaws. It shakes the penguin to break it apart. Then the seal eats its **prey**.

Leopard seals shake and slap their prey against the water to kill it.

FAST FACT

Sometimes pairs of seals work together to tear their prey into pieces.

CHAPTER 2

LEOPARD SEAL BODIES

Leopard seals are **mammals**. They can grow to around 12 feet (3.7 m) long. Their long, thin bodies have dark spots.

Some leopard seals weigh more than 1,100 pounds (500 kg). Females are usually larger than males.

Leopard seals mostly live in or near Antarctica. This **habitat** is very cold. A layer of **blubber** helps the seals stay warm.

NORTH FOR THE WINTER

Some leopard seals travel to warmer places during winter. Most go to islands near Antarctica. Some go to New Zealand or Australia. Others don't migrate. They stay in Antarctica.

Leopard seals are some of the largest hunters in the Antarctic region.

Leopard seals spend about a third of their time on land.

In the water, leopard seals' large flippers help them move. On land, leopard seals are slower. They must flop on their bellies to move.

FAST FACT
Leopard seals can swim more than 25 miles per hour (40 km/h).

CHAPTER 3

UNDERWATER HUNTERS

Leopard seals are **carnivores**. They catch and eat many types of animals. Their diet includes fish, penguins, and other seals.

Leopard seals can swim faster than penguins. That helps them catch their prey.

Leopard seals also eat krill. These small animals float in ocean water. To catch them, seals swim with their mouths open. Their back teeth catch the krill as water runs past.

FAST FACT

A leopard seal's front teeth are long and sharp. They help grab large prey.

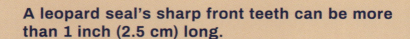

A leopard seal's sharp front teeth can be more than 1 inch (2.5 cm) long.

Leopard seals almost always hunt alone. Sometimes, they eat together. They may also steal one another's food.

A seal's whiskers help it sense movements in the water.

Strong noses and good eyesight help leopard seals find their prey.

STRONG SWIMMERS
Leopard seals usually hunt in shallow water near sheets of ice. But they can dive to 1,000 feet (305 m). And they can stay underwater for 15 minutes at a time.

CHAPTER 4

LIFE OF A LEOPARD SEAL

Adult leopard seals spend most of their time alone. But they come together to **mate**. To find partners, they sing underwater.

Leopard seals are sometimes territorial. That means they defend their area from other animals.

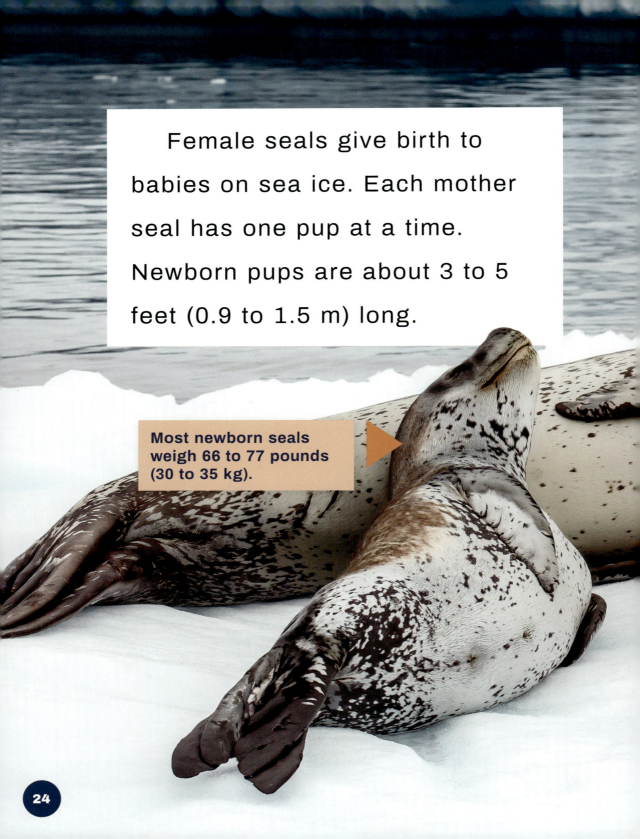

Female seals give birth to babies on sea ice. Each mother seal has one pup at a time. Newborn pups are about 3 to 5 feet (0.9 to 1.5 m) long.

Most newborn seals weigh 66 to 77 pounds (30 to 35 kg).

CHANGING HABITAT

Climate change is melting ice in Antarctica. That means leopard seals could lose safe places to raise their pups. They could also have trouble finding enough food.

At first, pups drink milk from their mothers. After a few weeks, they begin to catch food. Finally, a few years later, the pups become adults.

FAST FACT

Leopard seals usually live for about 26 years in the wild.

Young pups stay on ice or land. Their mothers feed them and teach them to hunt.

COMPREHENSION QUESTIONS

Write your answers on a separate piece of paper.

1. Write a few sentences explaining how leopard seals hunt their prey.

2. Leopard seals live near Antarctica. Would you want to visit there someday? Why or why not?

3. How long do seal pups take to become adults?
    - A. a few weeks
    - B. a few months
    - C. a few years

4. Why do leopard seals usually hunt in the water instead of on land?
    - A. Their prey moves faster in the water.
    - B. The seals can't move as fast in the water.
    - C. The seals can't move as quickly on land.

5. What does **migrate** mean in this book?

Some go to New Zealand or Australia. Others don't migrate. They stay in Antarctica.

    A. eat different foods
    B. move to a new place
    C. rest during one season

6. What does **diet** mean in this book?

They catch and eat many types of animals. Their diet includes fish, penguins, and other seals.

    A. what an animal sees
    B. what an animal hears
    C. what an animal eats

Answer key on page 32.

GLOSSARY

blubber
A thick layer of fat.

carnivores
Animals that eat meat.

climate change
A dangerous long-term change in Earth's temperature and weather patterns.

flippers
Flat body parts that animals use for swimming.

habitat
The type of place where animals normally live.

mammals
Animals that have hair and produce milk for their young.

mate
To form a pair and come together to have babies.

prey
An animal that is hunted and eaten by another animal.

TO LEARN MORE

BOOKS

Humphrey, Natalie. *Leopard Seal vs. Cougar*. New York: Gareth Stevens Publishing, 2023.

Juarez, Christine. *Antarctica: A 4D Book*. North Mankato, MN: Capstone Publishing, 2019.

Sommer, Nathan. *Tiger Shark vs. Leopard Seal*. Minneapolis: Bellwether Media, 2023.

ONLINE RESOURCES

Visit **www.apexeditions.com** to find links and resources related to this title.

ABOUT THE AUTHOR

Marissa Kirkman is a writer and editor who lives in Illinois. She enjoys reading about animals, science, and history. Her favorite animals to learn about are sea animals.

INDEX

A
Antarctica, 7, 12–13, 25

B
blubber, 12

C
carnivores, 16
climate change, 25

F
flippers, 6, 15

H
hunting, 7, 16, 20–21

I
ice, 4, 7, 21, 24–25

K
krill, 18

M
mammals, 10
mate, 22
migrate, 13

P
penguins, 4, 6–8, 16
prey, 8–9, 16, 18
pups, 24–26

S
swimming, 15, 18, 21

T
teeth, 18

ANSWER KEY:
1. Answers will vary; 2. Answers will vary; 3. C; 4. C; 5. B; 6. C